MAKING A LIVING

Also by Rosalie Moffett

Nervous System
June in Eden

MAKING A LIVING

Poems

ROSALIE MOFFETT

MILKWEED EDITIONS

© 2025, Text by Rosalie Moffett
All rights reserved. Except for brief quotations in critical articles or reviews, no part of this book may be reproduced in any manner without prior written permission from the publisher: Milkweed Editions, 1011 Washington Avenue South, Suite 300, Minneapolis, Minnesota 55415.
(800) 520-6455
milkweed.org

Published 2025 by Milkweed Editions
Printed in Canada
Cover design by Mary Austin Speaker
Cover artwork: "Oval Right," plastic detritus collected from Kehoe Beach, by Richard Lang and Judith Selby Lang
Author photo by Jacob Sunderlin
25 26 27 28 29   5 4 3 2 1
First Edition

Library of Congress Cataloging-in-Publication Data

Names: Moffett, Rosalie, author.
Title: Making a living : poems / Rosalie Moffett.
Description: First edition. | Minneapolis, Minnesota : Milkweed Editions, 2025. | Summary: "A brilliant, lithe collection making space for the resolve and hope of motherhood amid consumerist dreams and nightmares"--Provided by publisher.
Identifiers: LCCN 2024030325 (print) | LCCN 2024030326 (ebook) | ISBN 9781571315656 (trade paperback ; acid-free paper) | ISBN 9781571317896 (ebook)
Subjects: LCGFT: Poetry.
Classification: LCC PS3613.O366 M35 2025 (print) | LCC PS3613.O366 (ebook) | DDC 811/.6--dc23/eng/20240712
LC record available at https://lccn.loc.gov/2024030325
LC ebook record available at https://lccn.loc.gov/2024030326

Milkweed Editions is committed to ecological stewardship. We strive to align our book production practices with this principle, and to reduce the impact of our operations in the environment. We are a member of the Green Press Initiative, a nonprofit coalition of publishers, manufacturers, and authors working to protect the world's endangered forests and conserve natural resources. *Making a Living* was printed on acid-free 100% postconsumer-waste paper by Friesens Corporation.

For Marianne

Contents

Resolution   1

/

Failure to Appear   5
Forsythia   6
#Blessed   8
Hope   9
No Wonder   10
Omen   11
A Prophecy Is Nothing   12
Hope   15
Will   16
The Pea Shoots with Their Thin Tendrils   17

//

Making a Living   21
Make-Believe   24
A Prophecy   27
Time and Place   28
What Is There   32
Total Liability   33
Failure to Appear   35
Safe   37
Hysterosalpingography   39

///

Absence, like Emptiness   45
Happy   47
Equation   48
Total Liability   50
Transfer of Power   52
Hawks   54
Nest Egg   55
Making a Living   57

////

Transfer of Power   61
Resolution   62
Shriek Mark   64
Redeem   66
Hope   68
Word   69
Making a Living   71
Cathedral   73
This Landscape   74

Acknowledgments   77

MAKING A LIVING

RESOLUTION

Cold morning, unadorned.
   The Dollar General employees
at work in their carbon
   footprint nightmare. I avert my eyes
from the perpetual feed of koalas
   in brush fires, from the leftover Christmas
memes chiding the Christians about children
   in cages at the border. We tore out a new page
to make resolutions dedicated to taking
   the next step in our lives. Number 1: *Make a baby.*
2: *Make an appointment to get the cross-*
   shaped IUD removed. My husband may still fear hell
but the idea was never anything
   but comical to me—some other place
to suffer? Fires in Australia engulf fairy-tale
   animals, children sleep on concrete
in space-blanket bedrolls. I sit by a window,
   one clear layer in, Googling the price
of baby monitors, of doorbells that convey all
   they see to a smartphone. Who can bear
to look at the world?
   Deep down I'm just like everyone,
obsessed with dreaming
   up the future, with hell, with all
that spares us
   the act of looking away.

FAILURE TO APPEAR

The hawk
aloft and stock-still
cuts itself

free from the sky's talons
to fall. The small mole
loses hold

of one world. Pull one
burr loose, its hooks
now useless.

Do this again

and again—
each bush

of longing
accounts for loss.

FORSYTHIA

will forever remind me
   of my mother stealing
branches of it outside the DoubleTree Inn
   in Murfreesboro, Tennessee
for her mother's funeral. Cinder-block-strip-mall
   side of town we'd gone to for Starbucks,
caffeine fortification and an OfficeMax
   to print the programs. That's one facet
of the end: your family scrounging the city-side
   for something pretty as tribute under the eyes
of Ruby Tuesday patrons. Here I am,
   still young, young-*ish*, no kids, perched
in the bland middle swath of my life, wondering
   what I'll pilfer for my own mother's ceremony.
Her own purple irises, perhaps. Or, if in winter,
   the prickly stalks of thistles, brown
and old but holding magnificent
   crowns of snow: translucent sculptures
of time I'm taking from some future to let
   melt in my present embrace of eventual grief.
Each moment I poach just repopulates.
   Something borrowed is the standard rule
for weddings; something stolen, my new protocol
   for funerals. Here I am, young, *my whole life
ahead of me!* I shouldn't dwell on any of this.
   It's the start of spring. Everyone is still alive.
Everyone, within reason. The yellow
   branches of forsythia are fireworks shedding
bright sparks in piles on the parking lot.
   There's a Starbucks nearby, no matter where I go.

There's a big box store, a row of measly
  ornamental shrubs, a tree or two.
There's the present where everyone lives, now
  studded with moments I've robbed from a time
I imagine, in which a child watches me scavenge
  the landscape for bits of beauty,
learns how to do it herself.

#BLESSED

In my flower bed, I hesitate to be delighted by everything I have worked for in my tiny territory in the heartland of America, where the memes are good enough to be Band-Aids

for suffering, the memes are of '50s housewives saying, *I'm ready for some blessings that* aren't *in disguise*, and where still more daylilies have opened into paroxysms of orange so orange

it hurts. The grocery's florist gives a short lecture on pain: to stay alive, blooms require fresh cuts. I imagine you asking what no child would ask: *What does this prove?* The lilies echo

the solar explosions a paintball makes on a surface. #Blessed is a yellow decal pressed on our neighbor's front door. Hose nozzle hissing in my hand, I recall my high school French:

Je suis blessée. I am hurt. Once, it was a blessing to be close enough to be splashed by the blood of the sacrifice. To *look* wounded. Hence the word. Small bloom of dull red blood—

This morning, all I want is to look unharmed, to know you were meeting me at the mouth of this world. What to call that feeling in the mind like a magnet pulling toward the fridge?

Blessing inches toward *blessure*. A green beetle hovers above the speckled throat of a lily. My longing unfolds like a pocketknife. I am so close to answering you.

HOPE

Once thought to dwell in silence,
snakes allow sound

in through their jawbones,
the ground's vibrations
traveling into the skull.

Landlocked in the Midwest,
I set aside the shallow shell

whose scallop shape
produces no shadow sea
against the ear.

I begin again to forgive
my oracular wrongs.

NO WONDER

In the Fertile-Focus microscope, I see
the soldered wires connecting the light to its switch
are loose when I disassemble the tube
to examine its limited innards. Something gone

a little wrong in the construction. Simple fix,
though you'd think such a product more careful
with omens. The highway billboard is visible
from my second-floor window only in winter

when the trees seem dead. *Your Wife Is Hot* it says
and pitches, in modest font, a new HVAC, aching
in its faded-saffron background: small summer all fall
persisting in the dimensions of the sign. It's no wonder

we struggle to pry past from present. The spit I put
on the glass slide dries, as directed, for five minutes.
When I return, no discernable fernlike patterns
which means, in the language of the microscope, No,

I won't be growing anything anytime soon
inside me. In remedy, I do my detox-flow yoga, or sit
awestruck, as the car is ratcheted through the Splash
N Dash automatic car wash. No understudy heart

starts up like a cricket in the basement. I persist
in imagining mine as a thing cut
from red paper folded in half. So flimsy,
though who can blame me?

OMEN

From the firewood pile, I peeled up bark to marvel at the invasive ash beetle's mural of appetite: the chewed grooves, roomy chambers and egg galleries. Something bored through my soft pith. Engraved another banknote. We don't speak of it. Night before our wedding, elated, traveling the narrow canyon road. Then, in the pickup's lights: two black kittens. Him wrapping it in his shirt. Home with a dropper of milk, but it didn't last the night. Dead black cat in a shoebox. Debt cracking its coin-purse mouth. I zipped the white lace dress. Pinned lavender in my hair. How else to explain it? The future had tallied what I owed. I assumed the currency was misery. That I was wrong didn't matter. I began to stockpile. He wanted to know if the marriage would hold. This was later. If we couldn't—did we say it—have a child. I felt that to answer *yes* would reduce my investment. Faithful pupil in America's immersion school of *you must pay for what you want,* I paid. But I couldn't keep the hope out. The thought I might show a child the beautiful grooves, the breathing hole the beetle makes in the bark, entered like the beetle itself. And then the thought did what someone else, prying, might think was marvelous.

A PROPHECY IS NOTHING

without the fulfillment of what was foretold.
The mind, pried from another sleeping
pill's glue, in the screen's blue light, choosing
among visions. Who knows me
as the search bar does, which holds
sacred its grasp of me
as a creature of habit?

The iconography of the magnifying glass
as if to better see something
kept from the naked eye—

I understand magic to be a series of steps
denied the viewer. From the house, small items
kept vanishing: foil-wrapped candies, keys.

Some curatorial spirit in the walls. Search results
of purchasable metal snap-jaws, or the escape room
-style live traps spread before me in a grid
like a tarot reading. My own small prophecy
plus the code one is told to keep
to oneself from the back of the credit card

sent deep into the circuitry of conveyor belts: the heart
of the fulfillment center. I understand prayer
can be traced to the first need
for help from an entity greater and more capable
than the self. Amazon never sleeps. Amazon closes,
as if pulling tight a black

suture, the distance between desire
and the fulfillment of that desire. I was promised
full control. I was promised *minimal risk
of false triggers or stolen bait.*

*

It is a mistake to regard the pack rats
as akin to those hoarders featured on TV.
A rat would never save
what it could, at any moment,

eat. Theirs is a desire for beauty.
This, like the pair of silver earrings
of which one remains in my possession, we share.
Rat that has its house inside my house and inside its house
my things. No one wants a thinking to be taking place
inside their thoughts, and that's how it feels.
The stars fill by small fractions

in the 5-star rating. Fate is still
their purview: a horoscope to narrow
what once seemed an infinite field of will. Don't think
it's a coincidence, the aural overlap of *prophet*
and *profit*. The highest-reviewed trap is said to furnish
a humane end, thanks

to the above-average speed of the mechanism.
The highest-reviewed trap arrives promptly on my doorstep.
Researchers know pack rats make trades: e.g., whether to drop
what they already carry for some new treasure
in their path, placed there

by an unseen hand. It's so easy these days
to receive what you thought
you needed while in night's emporium
of urgencies—the multitude self-populates

with algorithmic precision what it thinks
you'll want. What may work best as bait.

HOPE

When empty
-handed, I lifted my shirt

to make a hammock
beneath a tree I did not mean

to find
on a median, in a park, anywhere

I found myself
without receptacle, reaching

for instance for those
mulberries that look

like mulberries
but do not have a taste and do not

let a fabric forget them.
I could not refuse

an offering. I could not
refuse even that

which I found
unpalatable.

WILL

Blank cartridges, useful in races, threats, theater,
and reenactments—all heat lightning, no rain. Vacant silo
slotted into a barrel. As silly as near beer or decaf
I had no need of. I toppled bottles off the roof

of the defunct diesel Rabbit with a pearl-handled pistol
as a kid in a meadow. My good aim, even then. Now,
the onesie I stumble across on Etsy: iron-on assault rifle
and *Proof my daddy doesn't shoot blanks*. Peach tree, blue-green
magpie flash, the creek's little song. Proof enough of what

the world can hold. Atop the tractor, I mowed the meadow
towing the Bush Hog, backing into brambles like God
making a new topography, everything bending
to my will. The two senses of *will* in rapturous collapse:

what you want and *what you'll get*. In the will is the pistol, cracked
windshield and Bush Hog. In the will is the meadow, empty
in its barrel of trees. Branches clotted with small green peaches.
Dip a dropped one in creek water and the fur turns silvery

like a mirror. Little miracle. Proof of something
looking one way, being another. What carnage
did he acknowledge, who coined the term *shooting
blanks*? What far-off creature drops from the money
shot when using, so to speak, *live ammunition*?

That failure of the will never so clear
as when the bottle remains whole and still.

THE PEA SHOOTS WITH THEIR THIN TENDRILS

grope for the solace some seek in church
or nature, stable rung to lay their weight
and lift it toward the light at the top
of the trellis to lure their white apparitions,
blooms floating in overnight in the dew
while below slugs succumb to my strewn iron
pellets, primordial succumbing to mineral. I swallow
each morning ovular prenatal pills like taxes
for services not rendered. My brother refused to eat,
as a boy, peas, *their wrinkled faces*, their tendency
to be broken under spring's interrogation,
made to speak in their language of need
for light, for water, for one to scatter
bait at their feet and undo the hunger
that rivals their hunger.

II

MAKING A LIVING

I had imagined thread
to stitch myself more
tightly to this world.

   What is it
I needed? To pull you

through the eye of a needle.
To be the needle, able

to pierce time. I wanted to hold it in place.
Without which days had begun to pour
themselves out in the sink.

Something was emptying. Something was beginning

to feel flimsy. The country was sick and full
of bright, hollow shapes. Off-limits
McDonald's PlayPlace still lit at dusk like a snow globe
in the distance. *What do you think of that*,
   I was saying to you.

There I was, teaching plot, explaining *the protagonist
must act*. Oh, I was making
   a living

   like this.
And time was passing

and nothing was happening. This is a dull story.
My heels in the stirrups and on the stirrups
little socks advertising Enfamil.

A woman with a wand
gave me a tour
of my interior, strange roil
  of black static.

What do you think of that,

I was saying to no one. And

by *that* I meant everything.
  Sharp breath

of cold air between car and front door,
a marriage, a bank account, the mind's
unwillingness to stop

  making little towers
  of words.
How was it not enough

that had always been enough? Some message
finally arriving

as if a bill forwarded from a past address:
my life was not a whole. Not the fence,

but a post. Not the coat,
long, luxurious, warm,

but a pocket. My hands patting
   the place
where I thought

something should be.

MAKE-BELIEVE

Mostly dumb, but hens are finely tuned
to length of days, won't lay in earnest
till after the equinox, sliver of additional light
they measure from their mud-yard,
heads cocked to the sky. Same gut process, spin
of tumblers unlocking a stock of promise I feel for
and find nothing. If not instinctual calculus, the hens
perhaps receive a sign from a deity whose mythos
is beyond us, who allows the smallest
her status, her neck defeathered and red
from pecking. Hierarchical order made here

evident and cruel by the confines of the hog wire,
but flourishing in tree-lined neighborhoods,
their school districts, government and factory chains
of command in supposed exchange for the comfort
that some higher-up, snug in his pay grade, is taking
care of the coyotes or skunks, the exterior
threats who menace the edges. Calling god *the Man*

Upstairs makes god a boss, his office like all boss offices,
beyond reach, from which he chomps a cigar, orders
a new cumulonimbus, indulges his odd interest in the innocent
girl from my high school tennis team who called him
that, who pinned her wins on her daily memos
unto him. Unlike some birds with their museum

-quality architectures, chickens just scratch
a divot, deposit in it their contribution to the future
of bird-kind. You see when you butcher a chicken

the row of yolks awaiting their containment
like cars on an assembly line: soft stuff of center
console, seats and steering wheel, and then the shell
is built around it. Not, as I once thought, a hollow vessel

made, then filled. SUVs exist that sense in forward
or reverse an approaching car, that brake and steer
within the painted lines, in whose ads
children asleep are safe in the back seat. No such thing

when I was young, when ads were telling us
*This is your brain. This is your brain
on drugs.* Whole egg, egg cracked
in the skillet and sizzling,
as if the perfect analogy could cure all ills. I filled
the skunk's tunnel with rocks, thinking *Let's see him
dig through this*, and in the morning he had
simply dug a new tunnel, adjacent. Fresh mess
of blood and feathers in the henhouse. I'm that dumb

sometimes. I do my best. Sequester the poor henpecked one
to eat in peace, though I know it makes me soft
to care, to name her. I care. I name her, the one
I've come to imagine is holding out for me
to turn into a safer vessel: softer, spacious,
emptied of my petty cruelties. Nightly

the mistakes I'm afraid I'll make again
bloody each other in their confines.
My past scorn for the tennis girl who prayed
for something I believed

to be, in the grand scheme, *trivial*,
paces the hog wire. My own trivial yolk

keeps waiting in me for a better me before
she'll don her protective shell, allow herself
to be made. Prayer it might be called, to conceive

crudely of her shape and judgment, to fear myself
unworthy, unable to drag my *sorry* over the long table
I've been eating at. Mind a mud-yard, my hens mean
and reverent, they can't help it, they're helpless
and so what else is there to be.

I've long known all minor remedies
are mine alone, the vitamins, the timing, no divine
hand leads cord from socket to fire up
a heat lamp, no faux sun can fake my equinox—the boss
is me, little yolk, it's just me. I do my best. Ice-crust
on the water trough thin enough
to see through, relentless presence of windows
the world makes but no sign of the sign
I know not to look for but look for anyway. What is it
I thought would be shown me? Little face
discernible in a thin moon, lunar mirror

sending the sun's glimmer to the water, white plate
onto which I might, just by leaning over to look,
superimpose my own features, indulge a moment
of make-believe. Instead, the trough's dim metal bottom,
scrim of silt. Instead, that barb I keep
catching on, between two things, *make - believe,*
I want to be one.

A PROPHECY

This morning, the windowsill full
of roly-polies, those little military vehicles,
who've assumed, even in death,

their most defensive pose. *You can try to change,* the man
on the meditation app says, *the world,*

but it's much easier to change your mind. I study the armor
of small curved plates, their ingenious overlap.
Each, in its sphere, guards itself.
Last night, a possum, comatose in the garden.

Stiff, it can suffer in this state
no pain. This is essential. The dog, baffled.
Un-numbed, unharmed, the possum

ambled down the alley hours later. The world,
disinterested in itself, turns its attention
to my mind.

TIME AND PLACE

April and the yellow tulips elbow up
from their bed, faithful undead. Their even ranks
take over bank lawns and medians. As for me,
in this economy, I cultivate my aboveground

demeanor in order to find and retain employment,
something else bulking up at my root. With each
morning, spring has larded its cellar of darkness
with another night's harvest. The small architecture

in the dishwasher I attend to. I go for a long drive. The greens,
rampant, luxurious. Blue water towers stick their towns
like pins in butterflies. One billboard asks
Are you in a bad season of your life? Provides a hotline

which pipes in helpful scripture. Laughter,
one study found, like any other feeling, is just a tool

to simplify a difficult interaction.
How Midwestern. Here I am but I'm not
Midwestern. My generation, like a dropped jar
of ball bearings, lodged in the dark

cracks of the country's uneven floor. Where the job is
or was. Once, the rose, smoking in its frozen vapors,
was lifted from the liquid nitrogen, an apparition.
The science teacher, shattering it into shards

that skittered under our chairs. Our cheers, then,
sharp in the air. Clear only later, the point
of the lesson: something fragile had been made for us
more so and we cheered. All the while,

as we were growing up, weren't they,
who claimed the future was ours, burning it

around the edges to make it look a little more old-timey,
like a counterfeit treasure map, or a colonial reenactment of men
milling bewildered behind a door while a woman dies
in childbirth? In this economy, the tulips undress into nothing,

but then the irises start up. Foliage like swords. Grape soda
perfume. My preoccupation with what supplants what
in what order feels American. On the neighborhood app, everyone
complaining about Narcan. That it's whittling down

a needful darkness. They who bury the bulbs, who claim
to love this time of year and campaign for Christ to be returned
to the Easter basket. That the word *unfair* does not furl up
the great machinery of America's various Tilt-A-Whirls,

Ferris wheels, and shooting galleries, means language is working
for The Man. I can sympathize. Lately, to be alive is to listen

to mowers and whippers and blowers
and saws. The electric company's been at it
all week, limbing extravagant trees into a cut-hair
kind of mourning. Now, the power lines

march around the park with their bodyguards of air.
A man rakes a pile of pink petals toward the storm drain
and then it rains and rains until the basement walls weep.
I have a small shameful drawer of keys whose purpose

is lost but which I keep and keep. What I thought
was a feeling, I find in my hand as I see if it will fit
any of the locks in the long corridor made this way
by every moment leading up to this one. Joy

seems always to fashion another longing. Humans
are the only animals to use a tool to make a tool.

WHAT IS THERE

is not there
except in minimal sketches:

a road made of two
blue stripes, or
a four-paned window, or

what you start with
when drawing nothing

but the sky
touching the earth: single
horizontal line. Blue because

Clearblue is the brand.

TOTAL LIABILITY

Having avoided studying supply
and demand, etc. I swam, nonetheless, in an ocean
of economics, of finance law, unaware. Recall
    that old joke, one fish
to another: *How's the water?*
To which: *What the hell is water?* It's unforgiving

on the complexion, fluorescence. A tactless friend
in the grocery aisle: *Is this a bad time?* Each one is
    clear, almost ethereal,
but not so the whole, the roll of plastic produce bags.
    Clocking out, clocking in.
Something growing thin
as hours are torn away, then days. I pay

down my liability but it resurrects each month
like punched dough. I use my finest
French aloud each time I write *mort*
-gage on a memo line. On the local pond, a carpet
    of vegetation appears

solid. I know better. Those who don't
study the natural world inhabit something
    they barely grasp
the shape and depth of. I spend a little
time considering irises. Who has paid them
to mine the minerals, to assemble
this splendor? The labor of clouds, their shoulders
to the inching load of cold air—such a thought
clears the mind

    for a new development.
Each acre of broken ground, an open
invitation to invasive plants, which bend

to the market forces of investment,
production, and distribution and which choke
    almost anything you might save
up to buy, in plastic pots, from the nursery.

FAILURE TO APPEAR

Neighbors, evicted, spin the bald tires of a pickup in the yard-mud, iffy load lidded with a futon. Then they're gone, the lawn a not-lawn now and a box like a tiny hotel safe hangs from the doorknob.

No one recalls being born or seems to long for what it was before memory finally gained purchase on the slick surface of a lot leased us by an agency too distant to drop a check, too anonymous to hold in a single idea. This is clear

from the growing stack of doorstep church flyers, their large range of notions. Lot: a span of days, nights. This is it. AC unit clinging to the sill like a tick, clot of hair in the drain.

Lot as in *luck*. Sliding the quarter through the slot in the hardware store gumball machine, getting what you got. No backsies, the coin as gone as the key in the realtor's box. Future, what lands in your palm: hollow, varnished, sweet

just briefly but encoded with a need to keep it going long after it's gone tough and tasteless. The neighbors towed themselves free with someone's uncle's SUV and then were gone. *Agency* as in power, as in deciding your life. They lied and said it was theirs, that they were selling it, and then it was

so trashed a gutting crew came in with crowbars. The before as strange as the after but *beforelife* isn't a word.

To be the grass someone's memory spins its wheels in, the globe brimming with gumballs, or the palm—but I'm not, maybe never. Some limit written into the lease, some sink conceding to the sledge. Wrecked fiberglass tub in their front yard like a pulled tooth with roots. The neighbors had them young, they're still young, and me, empty and out of place. Godless and childless in the Midwest. There, wherever they are

is what they got: new lot, their toddlers and truck, their patched box spring. It's not that I think it's all luck. They have their mugshots and Failures to Appear publicly available on the internet. They were fine neighbors. Quiet, mostly. Not totally preordained.

Just that nothing can be undone. Each moment with its lockbox. Each year gutted for the next tenant.

SAFE

The news says the first baby's been born
from a deceased donor's womb.
    How will it feel years later to learn
of that cold and miraculous room?
My bet is no one will ask and perhaps not much
to say except, *Well, here I am.* Gratitude clings
    above the bus stop
in a tree, the Thank You–printed plastic bag
inflating, deflating, a wind-lung. On the screen,
    my pop-up ads: *Freeze your eggs
to be on the safe side!* The news says Gen Z is the loneliest
    and that loneliness is the same
as 10 cigarettes a day. The teens are breathing
the fumes of their bright, virtual world. The stream
    near my house is one I imagine
a child would love: tiny minnows, snails.
It's an odd polluted green. As a kid,
    I seldom ate sweet cereal,
and my mom made all our meals. Close calls only came
    later, in cars when I popped
pills whose provenance was mysterious, or escaped
houses of men who'd turned dangerous,
    though one claim to fame is I never
was lonely, just in a fantasy I marshaled
to be on the safe side. The viral news cycle dictates
I fixate on the border wall, kids in Walmart
    holding cells and the truth of Russian
nesting dolls: the egg of me having once been enclosed
in my mother, even as she waited

in her mother to be born. So now, knowing
>> myself to be a crowd, the next
two generations and I round the corner, tripping
the motion sensor in the freezer aisle, so *blip blip blip*
>> all the way down: a flickering-on of lights,
a dim little dawn. At all times, someone is shining up
>> something nice and false for us
>> to live in. I think frozen
>> pizza is a marvel.
I think there's nothing
truer to say than *Here I am.*

HYSTEROSALPINGOGRAPHY

> *A radiologic procedure to investigate the shape of the uterine cavity and the patency of the fallopian tubes.*

In ancient Rome, a haruspex didn't see the future
in the viscera of the sacrifice, just the mood of the gods,
their disposition. Even then, in the prediction,
a little wiggle room. In the room, the machine, maneuverable
from the ceiling, small sink. No place for my clothes. Sacrifice
tableau too boring for a painting. The liver we know
was of particular interest—the liver they thought

the maker of blood, the maker of life itself.
I bled through the napkin put there to be bled on.
The gynecologist showed up in her lead apron.
How we know what we know we owe to the bronze
livers recovered with their diagrams intact. That *recover*
means *to find* or *get better* rather than *hide* or *upholster*

seems a kind of test. My uterus, a knocked-out tooth
of dark dye on the X-ray. My fortune
to be born in this era of divination, all my insides
still on my inside. I was taught in school the fundus
was *the roof of the womb*, though in any house, any hollow
organ, it's just the part farthest from the opening.
The eye has one. The stomach. The sky

you might say is a blue ceiling and below,
doors to this world open along with shiny black exits,

unholstered. Flag ceaselessly half-mast. What good is it
to grope hopefully into the future? No one will recover

my X-rays from the earth. They're behind my patient
portal, password-protected entrance whose virtual cathedral
stretches back and back, but cannot be
stepped into. As with the air
above my home, there are limits to the ownership
of my prospects. The wide straight line of the freeway
sparks an expansive mindset. Exquisite fruit
on the Fig Newton package with the lesser thing enclosed.
Packaging, a failed CIA plot to inoculate
against letdown. I once thought a life was like an odd object
you inched out of a lake, knowing little by little more

what kind of thing you had, as I did
from the cheap motorboat, fishing up twisted
lumber mill rejects, propellers, or cattle skeletons.
But once it was clear what it was, it was easy
to let it slide back in. You can see why
I'm in need of a new thought. In need of what
insurance refuses to cover. The Statue of Liberty
quivers in a foreground conjured from the *Magic Eye* book
in the clinic waiting room. Like any promise
bucking a pattern, even a small softening
of resolve breaks it. Twitch away to the coverage

—or is it recoverage, or recovering—of another
shooting, phone footage and shouting, and the page regresses
to its cryptic scheme of fragments. The original appeal
of *Magic Eye* was in the disbelief in anything there
to see. My organs packed between the crescent moons
of my hips on the screen. One-room house with a roof.

The dye was to bloom out like smoke from two chimneys.
The present kept falling all around like rain, like questions
in a lengthy poll on my user experience
of this world, whether it was worth it

to cut free a door painted shut. Shouting and blood
in the footage, too much to let in. The mood of the gods
was sought via birds and entrails. Outcomes hiding there
like shapes in another dimension a special technique
—half-crossing of the eyes—calls into being.
The allure of this method, of any method
of divination, is that it turns us away

from what has been hauled, dripping, into the light.
The lake I'm remembering is a reservoir
made by the Army Corps of Engineers
who choked a river for its power. It holds its own moon
and everything anyone throws in. American museum
in the depths, unvisitable. It's just as well. After awhile
it must get easier to leave a door shut. To soften
all attention. I never made a promise
to this place. Let the nation stay
in its coverlet of myth. The water
upholstered in sky.

ABSENCE, LIKE EMPTINESS

has need
of a fixed area.
Of the dead, we know

they are not here.

Morning hauls it up
from the depths,
like a bubble, the dream

of you wobbling
as it rises
through the mind's green

aquarium,
bursting on the surface
of awareness

and without edges

it's nothing.
I watch from the icy field
an enormous menace

of starlings lift,
almost

solidify,
then dissipate.

*What on earth
are you doing*
—the church's

electronic marquee—
for heaven's sake?

Every cloud
is compelled at last to fall,

to rub the gray riverbed
like a cat against a leg.

Here, on earth
the river is a man

-made lake
dammed

and full
of thoughts,
slow and large:

the carp I saw
someone standing

in a boat shooting
with a crossbow.

HAPPY

In the Doppler weather app the weather
of the past is free but stops like a dog
against a hidden fence at the present. For a fee,
a switch can be flipped in the phone's brain
to let the storm crawl across the barrier
between known and foreseen, let it
clothe the tristate area in color-coded clouds.
There's a relief in releasing the whorl
to its desire, its projected desire, like unleashing
the dog into a field of geese and then the geese
are gone. Having made them rise and disappear
he is happy where they were. Everything's a prayer
anymore. Everything's the air into which
desire rises, scatters.

EQUATION

At the CVS with its liquor
secure behind the counter, the cashier
raised her eyebrow, said *Worried*

or excited? I took a pen,
in fifth grade, to my report card,
made every minus
into a plus.

A certain kind of person hates to fail a test.
There's a range of options.

For those suspicious of arithmetic,
the pricier Clearblue tests can tell you
in words what you want or do not want

to know, though some illiterate windstorm
will do the intolerable
math anyway: adding fat, dramatic clouds
then subtracting them back
into the imaginary

through a small slit—a minus sign
can take nothing

from nothing. *Hopeful* is what I said
and walked home

letting my breath out
where it appeared

in the frigid air
to precede me

like the idea of living
clearing my path.
I could already feel a new kind of love

using me
to calculate
an unfathomable sum.

TOTAL LIABILITY

Day one of Marketing 101 is *Don't sell a product.*
Sell an experience. Benjamin Moore's most
popular nursery shades are Forest Floor
and Polar Bear and furthermore,
      for lingering before Heron
and Muslin and Lichen, which fall
like snow in the paint display, I must
owe and owe. I know my time is money.
My home loan looms, laps its bowl
of sweat equity. Our local billboard rents
its loft of sky, offers me
      an idea of me
on a mountaintop, my bank's mobile app:
We're with you, wherever you are.
Having practiced on God,
on Fannie Mae, a certain facelessness comes easy
as a concept. Somewhere, someone, wanting.
      Money is nothing, given
the cloud. Anymore, you keep your card
as your bar tab grows, no wad of bills. A training
in the art of maintaining faith in the unseen.
      But there's a bulb lit
in my basement for which there is no switch
or beaded pull, a slow leak
in my bank account, it drips light—light
being one way money is made
      real to me.
Day two is product placement. I assume
each day, the sun, a wholesale retailer in the solar
pyramid scheme, releases some luminescence

to the down-line distributors. I wanted
what anyone wants, more
      than one life.
And now look at me,
glowing, growing round.
I hold my body
like a pen
poised over a check.
My windows spread their wares
on the floor.

TRANSFER OF POWER

Fetal kick and election season and everywhere
flags translate the direction of the wind
into arguments about the future. Each waiting
room's HGTV show revealing what's possible
to rip out: '70s carpet, floral wallpaper. Meanwhile
ads hawk a soothing formula for heartburn
utilizing America's language: the image
of an empty figure with a stomach
on fire. No mention of the heart, a fact
I am no longer surprised by, though isn't it
startling that everyone has something
lodged and jittering inside them
like a bead in a paint can
before some boring corporate surface
is transformed? My neighbor is alone
in his room of sound, the last privacy
he'll knit this season from the noise
his mower makes, a luxury captured in a number
of cut-grass Yankee Candle scents
marketed explicitly as such. The Last Mow,
then winter: a facade of white and light
and dark gray just begging
to be disfigured by a herd
of snowplows in a city whose ordinances
ban, among other acts of revision,
graffiti, though aren't we all harboring
a desire for some deviation
from the norm, some unlawful, in the spirit
if not the letter, transformation? American lawns
demand a countrywide prayer of penance:

the riding mower droning *stasis, stasis.*
I tell my students: *A character must want something.*
I tell them: *Make it something they can't have.*
Most of them want to make someone
realize just how wrong they've been
by the end. I walk home
past the power plant, its Elizabethan collar
of concertina wire, its small
authoritarian argument. *Like God, you decide*
what desire does to them.
A plant contorts slowly toward the light.
A character must change.
I spin it from the window, make the leaves
reach for me. Down the block a pickup
slumps on its flat tire. Prayer
brought about by nothing
more than the distance
from which it appears to kneel.

HAWKS

Their brown shapes in the brown-gray hills.
   As a child, I trained myself to see them
just so I could see them. Isn't that the system
   of fortune we embrace: to spot something
rare foretells good luck? Or is the luck the four
   -leaf clover itself, a scarce sight
its own blessing? Had I known,
   would I have spent those long hours sprawled
in the schoolyard, looking? I would've
   just imagined it: one green stem, leaf, leaf, leaf,
leaf. Yesterday, I held aloft the largest box
   of Lucky Charms I'd ever seen, like Moses
with the Ten Commandments. Bizarre excuse
   for marshmallows, and each misshapen, I know
from past disappointments, so
   I returned it to the grocery shelf.
My pleasures are limited to watching
   from the window of a school bus wending through
my memory's gray canyon, picking out the birds
   from the background they designed
themselves to disappear into. The longer
   I live the more past I have. I can say
now with certainty that I am fortunate
   to sit in this green chair, half-forgotten
glass of water near me, vision muffled by layers
   of daydream. I'm training myself to eye the landscape
of my interior, learning to make out
   the shape of a blessing: brown-gray silhouette
that pulls away, growing bit by bit
   smaller in the hills.

NEST EGG

Logging in to check the pie chart
of one's 401(k): boring miserly pastime
of the twenty-first century. No lovely clunk
of a gold doubloon, just Scrooge
and his TIAA-CREF password,
just Scrooge McDuck and his new bird-body.
My first time in Georgia it was August
and I was aghast at the snow
floating in the blue sky. (Hide your eyes,
McDuck, each time we find ourselves
driving in the wake of a chicken truck.)
Point is, most miracles
can be pinned on other people
amassing money in offshore accounts.
Once, I saw rocks light up on the bank
as the surf crashed in: true phenomenon
of phosphorescent plankton. Once, the power
went out in a packed stadium,
and the ring of stands fired up with that exact
blue-white plankton-light from flipped
-open flip phones. From above, there must've been
one shining eye in the pitch black
of the city. The pie chart
is a joke: it shows only what you have now
as if that's enough to illuminate enough
of a patch of the quiet dark
of the future. Oh, Scrooge, I know
the balm of a tall stack of coins. I, like you,
have a nest of fear. I like you best
as a bird. I read how domestic ducks

   neglect their eggs, which must be
     electrically incubated. Warm bulb which nursed
current from the wall-socket to make you
     take form, made you take all the currency and hold it
to the light to see if it could be changed
     from coin to mirror, from mirror to periscope
to peer into the unknown. Ah, Scrooge, it *feels*
     like it works, doesn't it? You were the first
to dip your spats into an Olympic pool
     of money—even as you dove, even as the children
rubbed, in disbelief, their fists across the dollar signs
     in their eyes, someone watched
the scales shift, felt the digits of the budget
     loosen their choke hold.

MAKING A LIVING

The factory's steam towers breathe their white into the clouds and I fear a child will think this the origin of all weather. The sky is empty, otherwise. It's Indiana, flat and poor. January. No sun, no crickets. In my car I tally the cigarettes I've seen today in their skittery dance on the expressway. Unsung ballet. Two fingers hang from a window in their particular posture of holding. Then, the letting go. Rehearsal of the disposal of trouble. The towers surrender their slow shapes. I know how clouds are made. Water is dismantled. *Vapor*, the taste of bubblegum or banana floating through a sunroof at a stop light. Vapor is water undone. Indiana, then the river, flat and brown, then Kentucky. No fireflies, no money. Crushed Styrofoam Polar Pop cup in every periphery. I breathe into the cold my own small clouds. What the factory makes, I don't know, but it makes its way into me. I'm afraid your sudden beauty will undo me. What then will I become? Above the new Costco, skeins of geese strung across the sky. On the display of discount flat-screens, more sky.

TRANSFER OF POWER

Sleep ate silent
holes in day

after day. I let it. I fed it
the softest hours, hovered

over the toilet, shallow
retch, no relief. Heart

burnt by lanterns lowered
with the jewels of my mind.

Magician in reverse: impossible
billow of silk swallowed

by the sleeve. This feeling,
a revel, reeling

you onto life's spool.
Nothing is pure. Wonder

is soft and woolen. Fear
has a pointed spindle.

RESOLUTION

Certain elements of isolation
were built into the design, given
the odds. This is made plain in the line

of cars in their evening
bed-ruffle of exhaust, idling
in the Rally's drive-thru

whose trademarked slogan is *You Gotta Eat*, as if
you might as well eat this.
The mind looks up

to the body. It has its aspirations, fashions
its own barriers. Barbed wire and fence posts
out past the last fringe of gas stations

and fast food. The snowy acreage
of choice whittling on all sides, a white pat
of margarine on the griddle. *Happiness*

is an inside job read not a therapist's office-door
decal but the marquee of a sparse motel
in which the occupants were stowed

like tablets in a half-empty blister pack.
The mind's inheritance is everything
the body lets in. It's difficult

to pinpoint when the inside began
to resemble the outside.
Wasn't once the country's soft carpet

rolling out in all directions? Now, a hall,
both walls pocked with shut doors. Small-town
motel I drove from at nightfall,

towing my condition
over the picked-through landscape
visible from the interstate.

Area so featureless and vast,
no distance seemed to close.
So be it. Look at it.

Each graffitied silo
and shotgunned road sign
might be decoded

to mean that you might
as well live this way, here.

SHRIEK MARK

Who among us didn't feel smug when learning
they pulled the to-be-mummy's brain through its nose
with a hook and tossed it, thinking the heart
the headquarters of all thought? Mine babbles on

from its lectern in almost-always iambic.
I hear it when it startles and pauses: cardiac fumbling
for punctuation. The exclamation point
was once the *shriek mark*, which shows how far we've come

in terms of diversifying our portfolio
of emotions, though in so doing, who knows now
if it's surprise or delight or anger
or fear, the inverted *i*, which is

the lowercase version of a capital *I*, which I know
means *first person*, i.e., a voice, a mind—and looks
like a tall, thin man, shoulders hunched under a brimmed hat,
the small, bareheaded *i*, a child—and I know

a child should arrive to our shared world
head down, should take a breath of strange
cold air, shock of awareness, imperative wail, the shriek
of a future pried free of my body, suddenly there

in every *!* each *!* holding in its slight shape all
feeling. Not a period. Not an end
but a grand finale, what had been one
audience, a single, collective thought

of music dispersing now into various concerns:
traffic, missed calls, the half-moon. A dandelion
late in its season realizing something
indescribable about the wind.

REDEEM

The sun was losing
a long gold tooth

on the linoleum
of the labor and delivery ward.

I lifted my plastic bracelet to the green eye
of the barcode gun and it sang

the first note
of money's national anthem.

Redeem, a word with its feet
in the cement block

of *bribe*, of *buy*. Each Tylenol,
a tiny egg in the nest

of the nurse's cupped hand,
rematerialized weeks later

on the itemized bill. Nearby, a sign
on the fine diamond storefront:

GOING OUT OF   SIN   !

Redemption, a mercy

of wind, of one idea
asleep in another.

I had been the nation
you lived in. Like a shore

in lapping water,
you made your borders

expand a little
with each breath.

HOPE

Smaller now even
than when you were born.

Asleep in the crook
of my elbow, pastel
swaddle. The window

I walk toward
then away from
then toward.

I imagine
it imagines
it has made
what it holds.

The full moon,
then a square
of empty black sky.

Then the outlandish dawn.

WORD

That it is the nation I lived in.
Wasp in its soft urn of fig.
The nights turned

colder, longer, less
fragrant. I should have
been painting what I thought

was the mouth
of each green fig
with olive oil:

an unsaid word
could be sealed in
and that word

would ripen the fruit.
I had read that before
forgetting it

before the light
frost fell, silver fur,
and too late

I recalled, I do not pray.
What word can you hold
until you yield,

weep syrup? The child
lived in the body
I lived in. Wasp

in the hollow. The frost.
The soft snow. Her voice.
What I won't say.

MAKING A LIVING

One cloud dragging its shadow
over the plowed field

like a child with a blanket.
Who could see this

and not understand what it meant
to feel everything had begun

to speak again? My longing
had been to know

what it would be to give up
the self that had grown hard

to hold, somehow larger
in its emptiness:

a bag my mind clung to
in a stiff wind, billowing cloud

pulled along above the field
it darkens. What is birth

if not silence
being turned into sound? I hear it

again. Joy spinning
the interior wheel

of its decoder ring, turning
every moment into an answer.

CATHEDRAL

In the yard, I kneel. Try to get the baby to say *iris*.
I believe this is within her abilities.
Hydrangea, no. *Azalea*, no.

The white flowers, delicate, strangely shaped.
Reminiscent of vertebrae

in the reliquary in the cathedral
in the city where I was alone,
able to say nothing but what I had

written in a small notebook: *Bitte hilf mir.*
Ich bin verloren. The echoes. The votives,
their small quivering flames. I shielded my eyes

as I reentered the sunlight and pushed through
the turnstile to the train, watched the scenery
of days, years, kept the candles
in their tiered holders lit

in my memory. One can't call herself
a cathedral, whose unlocked door

admits someone who sees herself
wavering in what is not
a birdbath and doesn't stop and wouldn't
know when to recite or kneel—

Iris, I say, tipping one toward her. *Iris.*

THIS LANDSCAPE

> *It is better to say, "I am suffering," than to say, "This landscape is ugly."*
> —SIMONE WEIL

is, though, isn't it? Within
the mirrored windows
multiplying the hospital's endless lot
I was given a scale of zero

to 10 for *the worst pain*
you can imagine, so one end
depended on the power of my imagination.

This, like a knife, I have
sharpened all my life so I could see
one future and then see it

pared down and down to almost
nothing. No one
had found anything

wrong in me, but so much was wrong
around me. Men invented war,
my friend called to tell me,
because they were jealous

of the bravery of labor, and the blood.
Then it was out of their hands.
Kudzu climbing the trees.
You spun your cells like cotton

candy into a small white cloud. You grew
dimensions of pain
I could imagine. Loss
unfolding, unfolding.
An infinite map

in the sliver of gold wax
already in your ear

when you made your first sound. I pushed you
in the stroller. I pushed you past the backside
of the U-Haul storage center, past the nest of sleeping bags

in the bushes beside Crazy Bob's Cajun Chicken.
This is what you dreamed
your way through. I could see it

through your closed eyes.
I was raw with the ugliness
I had imagined

would disappear
when I was relieved of my longing.

What a shame,
this landscape. What a relief
to see it.

ACKNOWLEDGMENTS

I offer my sincere gratitude to the editors of the following journals where these poems, some in much earlier versions, first found a home:

32 Poems: "Hawks"
Adroit Journal: "Equation"
American Poetry Review: "#Blessed," "This Landscape," and "The Pea Shoots with Their Thin Tendrils"
Code Lit: "Making a Living" [The factory's steam towers breathe their white into the clouds] (as "Exchange")
Copper Nickel: "Absence like Emptiness" and "Word"
Four Way Review: "Nest Egg"
Narrative Magazine: "Resolution," "A Prophecy is Nothing," "Failure to Appear" [Neighbors, evicted, spin the bald tires of a pickup], and "Transfer of Power" [Fetal kick and election season and everywhere]
New England Review: "Hysterosalpingography," "No Wonder," "Shriek Mark," and "Forsythia" (as "Petty Theft")
Pleiades: "Safe" (as "Saying the New Grace")
Ploughshares: "Total Liability" [Day one of Marketing 101 is *Don't sell a product.*]
POETRY Magazine: "A Prophecy," "Make Believe," "Transfer of Power" [Sleep ate silent], and "Redeem"
Poetry Northwest: "Will"
West Branch: "Happy" and "Time and Place"

I also would like to thank the past teachers who gave me, in many ways, my guiding lights, especially Mary Szybist, Don Platt, Marianne Boruch, and Eavan Boland.

And to the friends who heard drafts and who brought their intelligence to the evolution of these poems: Corey Van Landingham, Jacques Rancourt, Matt Morton, Edgar Kunz, Sam Ross, and Casey Thayer, thank you for your care.

To Daniel Slager and everyone at Milkweed Editions who has had a hand in making this manuscript a book, I appreciate your attentive and beautiful work.

Particular and enduring gratitude to Fady Joudah.

As always, everlasting love to my parents. And to my husband, Jacob, and to our daughter Marianne, who are at the heart of this book and at the heart of my heart.

ROSALIE MOFFETT is the author of *Nervous System*, which won the National Poetry Series Prize and was listed by the *New York Times* as a New and Notable book, and *June in Eden*. She has been awarded a Wallace Stegner Fellowship from Stanford University, and her work has appeared in the *American Poetry Review*, *POETRY Magazine*, *New England Review*, *Kenyon Review*, and *Ploughshares*. She lives in Evansville, Indiana, where she is an Assistant Professor at the University of Southern Indiana and the senior poetry editor for the *Southern Indiana Review*.

milkweed
EDITIONS

Founded as a nonprofit organization in 1980, Milkweed Editions is an independent publisher. Our mission is to identify, nurture, and publish transformative literature, and build an engaged community around it.

We are based in Bdé Óta Othúŋwe (Minneapolis) in Mní Sota Makhóčhe (Minnesota), the traditional homeland of the Dakhóta and Anishinaabe (Ojibwe) people and current home to many thousands of Dakhóta, Ojibwe, and other Indigenous people, including four federally recognized Dakhóta nations and seven federally recognized Ojibwe nations.

We believe all flourishing is mutual, and we envision a future in which all can thrive. Realizing such a vision requires reflection on historical legacies and engagement with current realities. We humbly encourage readers to do the same.

milkweed.org

Milkweed Editions, an independent nonprofit literary publisher, gratefully acknowledges sustaining support from our board of directors, the McKnight Foundation, the National Endowment for the Arts, and many generous contributions from foundations, corporations, and thousands of individuals—our readers. This activity is made possible by the voters of Minnesota through a Minnesota State Arts Board Operating Support grant, thanks to a legislative appropriation from the Arts and Cultural Heritage Fund.

Interior design by Mary Austin Speaker
Typeset in Bembo

Bembo was created in the 1920s under the direction of printing historian Stanley Morison for the Monotype Corporation. Bembo is based upon the 1495 design cut by Francesco Griffo for Aldus Manutius, and named after the first book to use the typeface, a small book called *De Aetna*, by the Italian poet and cleric Pietro Bembo.